D1592337

EARLIER AMERICAN MUSIC

EDITED BY H. WILEY HITCHCOCK
for the *Music Library Association*

20

THE PSALM-SINGER'S AMUSEMENT

THE PSALM-SINGER'S AMUSEMENT

Containing *A Number of Fuging Pieces and Anthems*

BY WILLIAM BILLINGS

NEW INTRODUCTION BY H. WILEY HITCHCOCK
Director, Institute for Studies in American Music,
Brooklyn College, CUNY

DA CAPO PRESS · NEW YORK · 1974

This Da Capo Press edition of *The Psalm-Singer's Amusement,*
published originally in Boston in 1781, was reproduced from a copy
in the collection of the Clements Library, University of Michigan.

Library of Congress Catalog Card Number 73-5100

ISBN 0-306-70587-7

Copyright © 1974 by the Music Library Association
Published by Da Capo Press, Inc.
A Subsidiary of Plenum Publishing Corporation
227 West 17th Street, New York, N.Y. 10011

EDITOR'S FOREWORD

American musical culture, from Colonial and Federal Era days on, has been reflected in an astonishing production of printed music of all kinds: by 1820, for instance, more than fifteen thousand musical publications had issued from American presses. Fads, fashions, and tastes have changed so rapidly in our history, however, that comparatively little earlier American music has remained in print. On the other hand, the past few decades have seen an explosion of interest in earlier American culture, including earlier American music. College and university courses in American civilization and American music have proliferated; recording companies have found a surprising response to earlier American composers and their music; a wave of interest in folk and popular music of past eras has opened up byways of musical experience unimagined only a short time ago.

It seems an opportune moment, therefore, to make available for study and enjoyment—and as an aid to furthering performance of earlier American music—works of significance that exist today only in a few scattered copies of publications long out of print, and works that may be well known only in later editions or arrangements having little relationship to the original compositions.

Earlier American Music is planned around several types of musical scores to be reprinted from early editions of the eighteenth, nineteenth, and early twentieth centuries. The categories are as follows:

> Songs and other solo vocal music
> Choral music and part-songs
> Solo keyboard music
> Chamber music
> Orchestral music and concertos
> Dance music and marches for band
> Theater music

The idea of *Earlier American Music* originated in a paper read before the Music Library Association in February, 1968, and published under the title "A Monumenta Americana?" in the Association's journal, *Notes* (September, 1968). It seems most appropriate, therefore, for the Music Library Association to sponsor this series. We hope *Earlier American Music* will stimulate further study and performance of Musical Americana.

H. Wiley Hitchcock

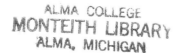

INTRODUCTION

William Billings (1746-1800) is the best-known of the large group of New England journeyman composers of the Revolutionary and Federal eras who wrote friendly, folkish choral music for "singing schools." From their beginnings in the 1720s, when Puritan ministers first organized them ot teach parishioners how to read notes and thus produce a more seemly music in praise of God, the singing schools developed into a universally popular social phenomenon by the Revolutionary period. Although the music taught in them was predominantly religious—settings of psalms, hymns, and anthems—the meetings of the singing schools were as much secular occasions as sacred, as much a social outlet as pious assembly. Billings and other singing-school masters wrote a rugged, homespun, social music accessible to the community at large; a music shared by all, rich and poor, young and old; a music as comfortable and familiar a part of everyday life as bean pots and New England rum.

The medium through which the "Yankee tunesmiths" taught their classes to read music by note and not to memorize by rote, was the tunebook, like the present one. Characteristically oblong in shape, thus sometimes called an "end-opener," and headed by some sociable title like *The Chorister's Companion, The Rural Harmony,* or *The Easy Instructor,* the typical singing-school tunebook was a how-to-do-it manual, with an introduction to the rudiments of musical notation and theory, and a what-to-do anthology of three-part or four-part choral music for performance.

Billings was the first of the New Englanders to produce such a tunebook, the *New-England Psalm-Singer* (1770) which contained 108 psalm and hymn settings and 15 anthems and canons; its title-page engraved by a fellow-Bostonian, Paul Revere. In 1778 Billings' *Singing Master's Assistant* appeared; aside from religious works, it contained a number of ardently revolutionary pieces, among them *Chester,* a favorite rallying song in the War for Independence. *Music in Miniature* (1779) followed; it mainly included reprints of successful earlier pieces. The present volume, *The Psalm-Singer's Amusement* (1781) was Billings' fourth publication. (It was followed by two more by this most prolific of the early New England composers.)

Perhaps because of the great success of *The Singing Master's Assistant,* Billings did not include in *The Psalm-Singer's Amusement* the usual instructive introduction on the rudiments of music, but simply referred readers to the earlier work which recently had been reissued. But the 1781 volume is unusual on another count, too: as Billings said, it was "not designed for learners," implying that its contents are more elaborate than was usual. And indeed, *The Psalm-Singer's Amusement* includes an unusually high proportion of anthems—substantially longer and more varied than the "plain" and "fuging" tunes which customarily predominate in the tunebooks of the singing schools. There are nine such anthems, as against four plain tunes (*Redemption, Mendon, Golgotha,* and *Resignation*) and seven fuging tunes (*Berlin, Framingham, Assurance, Emanuel, Wareham, Andover,* and *Adoration*).

Among the four other pieces in the book are two which must have been great favorites in the "singing assemblies"—concerts, essentially—at which singing-school classes displayed their musical prowess to the community. One, *Consonance* (not an anthem despite its subtitle), is a setting of a poem by Reverend Mather Byles, "On Musick," in which Billings graphically illustrates the imagery of the text in a technique of word-painting that goes all the way back to the Elizabethan period. The other, *Modern Music,* which begins with the lines "We are met for a concert of modern invention. / To tickle the ear is our present intention," is a naïve but engaging demonstration of "modern" American music, *circa* 1780.

H. W. H.

EARLIER AMERICAN MUSIC

EDITED BY H. WILEY HITCHCOCK

for the *Music Library Association*

20

THE PSALM-SINGER'S AMUSEMENT

THE
PSALM-SINGER'S AMUSEMENT
CONTAINING
A Number of Fuging pieces and Anthems
composed by
William Billings, Author of the Singing Masters Assistant
Printed and sold by the Author at his House near the white Horse
BOSTON 1781
J. Norman sculp.

ADVERTISEMENT

As this Book is not defigned for Learners, I thought it not effential to write an Introduction; but would refer the young Beginner, to my former Publication, entitled, "*THE SINGING MISTERS ASSISTANT*," which I have lately reprinted.

NB. This Work is a Part of the Book of Anthems, which I have fo long promifed; my Reafons for not publifhing the whole in one Volumn, muft be obvious to all who confider the prefent extravagant Price of Copper—Plate & Paper,—the Copper in fpecial if fo fcarce, that I don't think it poffible, to procure enough to contain the Whole, at any Price; befides if I was able to publifh the Whole, but few would become Purchafers, & I believe, that the moft will be of my Opinion, when I inform them, the Book could not be afforded for lefs than *TEN DOLLARS*. However, I hope that notwithftanding the prefent Difficulties, I fhall fhortly be able to publifh the Remainder at a much lower Price.

Berlin words from Dr W.

3

he dies   he dies   the heavenly lov...er dies the tydings strike a   doleful sound on   my poor heart strings

deep he lies in   the cold caverns   of the ground   come faints drop a   tear   or   two   on the dear bosom

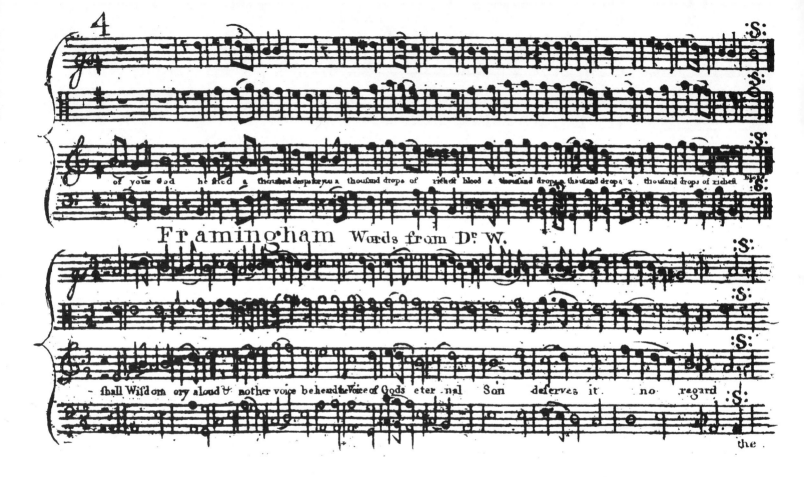

4

of your God   he shed   a thousand drops for you a   thousand drops of   richest blood   a thousand drops thousand drops   a   thousand drops of richest

Framingham Words from D.ʳ W.

- shall Wisdom   cry aloud &   mother voice be heard the voice of Gods   eter nal   Son   deserves it   no   regard

the

Affurance

Words from Dr W.

An Anthem

thou O God art Prai—is—ed in Sion art Prais—ed in Sion

the shall the Vow be performed

unto—the shall the Vow be performed in Jerusa—Jer

9

B

16 S. Allegro

Halleluiah · A men & Amen.

An Anthem 2d Samuel Chap 1st

the beauty of Ifrael is flain is flain upon thy high places how are the mighty faln how are the mighty faln

tell it not in Gath   tell it   not in   Gath

tell it not in   Gath tell it not in   Gath

tell it not in   Gath   publish it not in the   Streets of Asketon let the daughters of   the Philis tines rejoice

tell it not in   Ga   th

should rejoice & the daughters of the uncircumcised triumph & the daughters of the uncircumcised triumph

17

20

Redemption Words Anon.

th'Eter_nal speaks all Heav'n attends who that un_happy race defends . while Justice aims the Blow

see Nature trem..ble at their fate Death with his Iron scepter waits Hell opes her

24 An Anthem taken from sundry Scriptures for charity meetings

Blessed is he that considereth the poor the Lord will deliver him the Lord will deliver him

the Lord will deliver him in the time of trouble

Blessed is he that considereth the poor

Lord will preferve him & keep him alive the Lord

thou wilt not de

thou wilt not deliver him deliver him de

thou wilt not deliver him into the will of his enemies deliver him de

thou wilt not deliver him into the will of his enemies deliver him into the will of his

D

liver him &c.

liver him in to the will of his enemies :S: Piano

liver him

enemies Forte Blessed are the merciful for they shall find

mercy Blessed are the merciful the merciful for they shall find mercy

b key

he will repay it   the poor man cryd & the Lord heard him & deliverd & deliverd & de

liv·er'd him from all his trouble   a Father to the Fatherlefs the Widows God &

key

guide a Father to &c

pure religion pure reli

gion & unde filed before God & the Father if to vift the Widow to vift the

Widow to vifit the Widow & fatherlefs & to keep himfelf unfpoted to keep himfelf un

'S'

bleffed be the Lord

'S'

bleffed be the Lord God of

'S'

ipoted to keep himfelf unfpot ed from the World bleffed be the Lord God of Ifra el

bleffed be the Lord God of Ifra

33

key

mi is in A

neither to look thereon and one of the elders said unto me weep not weep not for behold the lion of the

tribe of Juda ye root of David hath prevailed to op--en the Book

& to loose the seven seals

38

& I beheld & lo in the midst of the Throne stood a lamb as it had been slain having seven
thereof

horns & having seven eyes which are the seven spirits of God sent forth into all the earth

& when he had taken the Book the four & twenty

& he came & took the Book out of the hand of him that sat upon the throne

the Angels were mute & they listned with wonder

Elders fell down before the Lamb

the Angels were mute

40

the Angels were mute & the saints they did shout did sho . . . ut did shout & sing worthy the

saint hosts did wonder

lamb worthy the lamb the lamb that was slain for he hath redeemed us for he hath redeemed us redeemed us to God & host

F

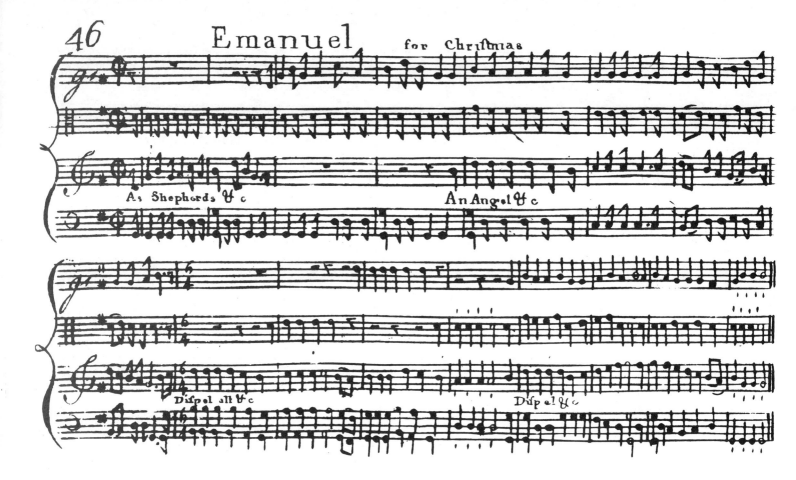

46 Emanuel _for Christmas_

As Shepherds &c

An Angel &c

Dispel all &c

Dispel &c

1st

As shepherds in jewry were guarding their sheep,
Promiscuſly ſeated eſtranged from ſleep;
An Angel from heaven preſented to view,
And thus he accoſted the trembling few

Chorus

Diſpel all your ſorrows, and baniſh your fears;
For Jeſus your ſaviour in Jewry appears

2d

Tho' Adam the firſt in Rebellion was found,
Forbidden to tarry on hallowed Ground;
Yet Adam the ſecond appears to retrieve,
The loſs you ſuſtain'd by the Devil & Eve.

Cho

Then Shepherds be tranquil this inſtant ariſe,
Go viſit you Saviour & ſee where he lies.

3d

A token I leave you whereby you may find,
This heavenly ſtranger this friend to mankind;
A Manger's his Cradle a Stall his aboad,
The Oxen are near him and blow on your God.

Cho

Then Shepherds be humble be meek & lie low
For Jeſus your Saviour's abundantly ſo

4th

This wonderous ſtory ſcarce cool'd on the Ear,
When thouſands of Angels in Glory appear;
they Join in the Concert & this was the theme
"All Glory to God & good will towards men

Cho

Then Shepherds ſtrike in join your Voice to the Choir
And catch a few ſparks of Celeſtial fire

5th

Hoſanna! the Angels in Extacy cry,
Hoſanna" the wondering Shepherds reply;
Salvation, Redemption are centured in one
All Glory to God for the Birth of his Son

Cho

Then Shepherds adieu we commend you to God
Go viſit the Son in his humble abode

6th

To Bethlehem City the Shepherds repair'd,
For full confirmation of what they had heard;
They enter'd the Stable with Aſpect ſo mild,
And there they beheld, the Mother & Child

Cho

Then make proclamation divulge it abroad,
That Gentle & Simple may hear of the Lord.

51

when shall I wake & find me there when shall I wake & find me there when shall I wake & find me there

Wareham Words from D.W.

thou art all in all for &c

My God my life my love to thee to thee I call I cannot live if thou remove for tho... thou art all in all

thou art all in all for &c

Mendom

Words from Relly

My Redeemer let me be quite happy at thy feet still to know my self & thee be thismy bitter sweet

look upon my infant state & with a Father's yearnings bless: dont thy ransom'd Child forget nor leave me in distress

54 Euroclydon An Anthem Psalms 107 for Marriners

57

Golgotha

Words from D. W.

my Ears attend the cry   where you must shortly lie

Hark from the Tombs a doleful sound   Ye living men come view the Ground

In spite of all your Towrs   Must lie as low as ours

Princes this Clay must be your Bed   The tall the wise the Revrend Head

Righteousness & peace have kissed each other

truth have met to gether

Fff Affetuoso

now is the hour of darkness come & Jesus waits to hear his doom the Roman speakes the Jews reply his blood be

on us   let him die :||: :||:   :||: his blood be   on   us   let him die :||: :||:   let him die

death & difpair what do I   fee the Lamb of God hang on a   tree with rufty   nails his body tore

& since we all a gree to set the tune onE the Authors darling Key he prefers to the rest

let the Treble in the rear   no longer for bear but expressly de

let the Counter inspire   the rest of   the Choir inflam'd with de si

let the Tenor suc ceed & follow   the   Le . . . ad till the parts are a   gree

let the Bass take the Lead & firmly proceed till the   parts are a   greed to   fuge a   wa

K

Treble time the Notes exceeding low keep down a while then rise by slow degrees the

process surely will not fail to please   thro Common &   Treble we

jointly have run weel give you their Efsance compounded in one all tho we are strongly at tach'd to the rest fir

four is the movement that pleases us best that pleases us best Six four is the movement that pleases us best

now we address you as Friends to the cause performers are modest & write their own laws altho we are sanguine

Clap at the Baristis the part of the hearers to clap their Applause to clap their Applause tis the part of the hearers to clap their Applause

78

A wake my heart arise my tongue prepare a tuneful voice in God the life of all my joys aloud will I rejoice

:S:
:S: in God the life of all my joys a loud will I re joice a
:S: in God the life of all my joys a loud will I re joice a loud a
:S: in God the life of all my joys a loud will I rejoice in God the strength of
:S: in God the life of all my joys in God the life of all my joys a loud a loud

Loud will I re..joi.....ce

:S:

will I re..joi...ce

:S:

all my joys aloud will I re..joice in God the strength of all my joys aloud will I rejoice

:S:

will I re joi ce

Adoration   Words from DW

& God the Spirit three in one   by all on

To God the Father God the Son   be honour praise & Glory giv'n

82

Car ear

Piano

with softer sounds in mild melodious maze Warbling between the Tenor gen

But if the Aspiring Altus Joins its force see like the Lark it wings its Towering coun

plays

83

Con.   1   S 2   85

their reſtleſs Race their reſtleſs Race till all the parts are join'd

Con.

then Rolls the Rapture thro the Air a

then Rolls the Rapture thro the Air a rou . . . nd in the full

then Rolls the Rapture thro the Air a round in the full mag ick melo

Rolls the Rapture thro the Air around in the full magic melody of ſound in the full mag ick

Forte   Con.

then Rolls the Rapture thro the Air around in the full magic me lo dy of found

An Anthem Isaiah 55 suitable to be sung at a Communion

Let evry mortal ear attend & evry heart rejoice the Trumpet of the Gospel founds with an inviting voice the

M

Fortissimo

21

Money without Money & without price

some buy wine & milk without

Money & without Price without Money & without Price

1:S:2

1:S:2

1:S:2

let him come let him come & take of the Waters of Li___fe freely 1:S:2 even so come Lord Jesus come &*t'll quickly

The Dying Christian to his Soul   An Anthem Words from Pope

Trembling hoping lingring flying

Vital spark of Heavnly flame

Quit oh Quit this mortal frame

100

Con.

Shut my sight

Steals my Senses

drowns my Spirits   tell me my

f orbs me quite   Draws my Breath

:S:

the World recedes   it   disappears   Heav'n

:S:

:S:

Soul can this be Death

:S:

the World recedes it

Hartford

Words from Kelly

103

Glorious Jesus Glorious Jesus thy dear name to praise this shall please us this shall please us greatly all our Days

Oh thy beauties how Divine how they in the Gospel shine holy Savior live for ever All our song be thine

Index

Tune's Names	Page	Beginning of Anthems	Page
Assurance	8	Thou O God	9
Andover	78	The Beauty of Israel	16
Adoration	79	Blessed is he	24
Berlin	3	And I saw	35
Emanuel	46	They that go down	54
Framingham	4	Who is this	63
Golgotha	61	Down steers the Bark	81
Hartford	103	Let every mortal Ear	89
Mendom	53	Vital Spark	99
Manchester	6		
Modern Musick	72		
Redemption	22		
Rutland	48		
Resignation	62		
Wareham	51		